An Institute for Pastoral Studies Publication

Other books in this series by Dr. Westerhoff:

A People Called Episcopalians
A Resource for New and Old Episcopalians

Holy Baptism: A Guide for Parents and Godparents
(and Adults to be baptized)

Grateful and Generous Hearts
A Stewardship Primer

This book is dedicated to my wife, Caroline,
with whom I have experienced the nature and meaning of
a Christian marriage and who is helping me to realize its purposes.

Table of Contents

First Thoughts

The Canons of the Episcopal Church require that before a priest can solemnize a marriage he or she must be sure that the couple to be married has been "instructed as to the nature, meaning and purpose of Holy Matrimony." This small book was written with this intent.

Marriage is both an event, the celebration and the blessing of a marriage, and a process, a couple's lifelong journey together. Marriage is an event that establishes a relationship and a relationship into which you will need to live. This small book intends to prepare you for the event and lay a foundation for the journey. At the event you will promise to travel together on a lifelong, sometimes difficult journey. There is much you will need to learn as you travel along, but before you make this life-transforming decision, it will be important for you to reflect upon and discuss the nature, meaning, and purpose of marriage.

I hope this book will provide a resource for and stimulant to these conversations between you and your priest.

Marriage Through the Ages

In primitive times a young man would capture a young woman from a neighboring clan or tribe and claim her as his wife. He was usually accompanied by another young man whose job it was to distract the woman's relatives or help fight them off during the abduction. In later times this person became known as the "best man." As time went on, fathers purchased wives for their sons, but the old ritual of abduction was now symbolized by the husband's picking up his bride and carrying her over the threshold of his home.

In the Greco-Roman world into which Christianity was born, marriage was a family affair. Women and children were considered property, and fathers therefore arranged marriages. Typically, the father of the groom gave a dowry to the father of the bride to compensate for a "property loss."

The marriage event was composed of two parts. The first was the betrothal, which took place at a family meal in the groom's home. At this time a promise of marriage at a future date was made, the girl was given a ring as a sign of possession by the man, and the dowry was exchanged.

Sometime after the betrothal, the second part, the marriage took place in the bride's home. The bride was dressed in a yellow dress with veil and a crown of myrtle, and she wore a cincture as a sign of virginity. She was delivered to the groom by a married woman, the pronuba, who acted both as a maid of honor and a representative of Juno, the god of home, family, and children. The contract was read and signed, and then the couple joined hands to finalize the relationship. Following a sacrifice to the family gods, the wedding feast was celebrated.

After the feast there was a procession to the husband's home. The pronuba would light the family fire, make a sacrifice at the family altar, prepare the marriage bed, and take off the bride's cincture and exit.

Jewish marriage rites were similar but without the pagan elements. In both Judaism and Roman society, marriage was a legal, contractual arrangement. When Jewish Christians married they used the same rite as Jews but made reference to Christ. When pagan Christians married, they followed the pagan rite but eliminated the pronuba and sacrifices.

Interestingly, for Christians singleness was as holy as marriage; some, in fact, would have said more holy. Marriage was for those who could not live a celibate life. The Christian community was to survive and grow through the conversion of adults rather than through the procreation of children. Therefore, for the first four centuries marriage remained a family affair and the church played no part in marriage.

Marriage customs began to change after the Christian church became the imperial state church. After two Christians had been married in a family ceremony, they would present themselves to a bishop or priest in order to receive a blessing. So it was that as long as the Roman Empire continued, the Church relied on the civil government to regulate marriages. In fact, this custom of the state marrying and the church blessing continues throughout much of the Christian world. The oddity is that in the United States, where we have an established separation of church and state, the church acts both on behalf of the state in performing marriages and on behalf of the church blessing them.

This blessing took different forms in the Latin-speaking West and the Greek-speaking East. In the West, where only one ring was exchanged at the wedding, it was known as the veiling of the bride and nuptial blessing. In the East, where two rings were exchanged, there was a crowning of both the bride and the groom.

New Understandings and Ways

The first major change in marriage customs took place in the tenth and eleventh centuries. With the collapse of the Roman Empire the church assumed a greater role in marriages. Now the priest was present at the groom's home for the ceremony. He witnessed the couple's mutual consent and the signing of a legal contract, the bride's pledge of obedience and submission to her husband, and his giving to her a ring. The priest would then bless the marriage and the marriage chamber where their union would be consummated and thereby made legal in the eyes of the church.

By the thirteenth century the marriage service as we now have it began to emerge. The betrothal and the marriage rite were united, and the first part was held on the outside porch of the church. The priest would first explain the church's understanding of marriage. Then the bride and groom were asked for their consent, and since there were few records, both those present and the couple were asked if they knew of any reason why they lawfully should not be married. Impediments were relation by blood or marriage, insufficient age, prior commitment to someone else (while they had to consent, some marriages were still arranged, especially for young children of noble families), incapacity to give consent, and undue influence.

Then insofar as the woman was still considered property, she had to be given away by her father. (One other change was that the bride's father now gave the groom's father the dowry, for he was assuming a financial burden.)

Once this part of the service was complete, the wedding party would go into the church and process to the altar where they entered into the marriage contract; the priest tied his stole over their joined hands (from which we get the expression "tying the knot") and pronounced them husband and wife; the bride's ring was blessed and placed on her finger; the priest blessed their marriage; and the couple exchanged the liturgical symbol of reconciliation, unity, the kiss of peace.

By the fourteenth century the whole liturgy took place in the church in the context of the Eucharist. During the reformation of the sixteenth century the Church in England became the Church of England and the first *Book of Common Prayer* (1549) was published. It contained a marriage rite that was a combination of Roman Catholic and Lutheran rites. There were a few other important and significant changes as well. Marriage was no longer a contract; it was now a covenant. Marriages were held during the parish Eucharist on Sunday. The dowry now took the form of alms for the poor. And the purposes of marriage were stated, namely to bear children, to provide a remedy against sin (the misuse of sex), and for the couple to care for each other.

Now in the twentieth century, while some of the theological under-standings of marriage have changed in the 1979 *Book of Common Prayer*, the marriage rite is fundamentally the same as that found in the first Anglican *Book of Common Prayer*. In our last section we will walk you through this contemporary liturgy and explain options you have and choices you need to make.

A Theology of Marriage

There are four major traditions within the Christian Church: Orthodox, Roman Catholic, Protestant, and Anglican Christian. The Anglican tradition, to which the Episcopal Church belongs, represents the one, holy, catholic, and apostolic church in England, which became the Church of England in the sixteenth century, and those churches around the world that owe their origin to the English church.

Our historic emphasis as Anglicans has been on the practical, as contrasted with the speculative, side of religion. We understand Christianity as a way of life, a matter of practice in which spirituality and morality, theology and ethics are one.

Fundamentally, Anglicans are Christians who worship according to some authorized edition of *The Book of Common Prayer* and are in communion with the see of Canterbury in England. Our primary identity is as a community of practice. That is, we are bound together by our liturgy. Orthodoxy for us is right worship rather than right belief. Our life of prayer shapes our beliefs and behaviors.

Through the years, in our constant quest to be faithful, we have revised *The Book of Common Prayer* and reformed our worship. This has often been painful and difficult because our liturgy is at the heart of our identity and is the basis for our theological and ethical convictions. To discover how we understand Holy Scripture and what we believe about issues of faith and life you need to turn to *The Book of Common Prayer* and engage in the process of interpreting this document. Therefore, to understand our theology of marriage we will reflect on the rite for the celebration and blessing of a marriage in the 1979 *Book of Common Prayer*.

The opening address in the marriage rite states first that marriage is a covenant and not a contract. Contracts are voluntary agreements that create legal obligations that are binding only insofar as both parties fulfill these obligations. A covenant, on the other hand, is a promise before God to enter into a relationship of love that is binding regardless of what the other does. It states that this bond and covenant relationship was established by God and blessed by Jesus to signify the mystery of the relationship between Christ and the Church. And it manifests itself as the union of two souls, which are composed of a body, mind, and spirit.

Continuing, this opening address states that the purpose of marriage is threefold: "for the couple's mutual joy; for the help and comfort given one another in prosperity and adversity; and, when it is God's will, for the procreation of children and their nurture in the knowledge and love of the Lord."

Mutual Joy
Webster's Seventh New Collegiate Dictionary defines joy as "an emotion evoked by well-being, success, or good fortune, or by the prospect of possessing something we desire." It is a state of happiness or contentment. But in Scripture joy has a more specific character: Joy is a consequence of our relationship with God and life in the reign of God.

We human beings have only one vocation, one calling, namely to live in an ever deepening and loving relationship with God and thereby with our true self (the self that is in the image and likeness of God), with all people, and with the natural world. This is also a description of life in God's reign.

The meaning and purpose of human life is to reach this end, an end that is both gift from God and our responsive action. We choose either marriage or singleness because we believe that through one or the other we can best fulfill our vocation. And we choose to marry a particular person because we believe that he or she, more than any other human being, will help us toward this end. The purpose of marriage, therefore, is spiritual. It is based on your conviction that life together will help you both grow and mature in your spiritual and moral life.

Help and Comfort
Webster's Seventh New Collegiate Dictionary defines help as "the giving of assistance or aid." It defines comfort as "the imparting of cheer and strength." But once again, Scripture uses these words differently. Help is used interchangeably with agape or charity love, that is, love as an act of the will that seeks the other's good or well-being. Comfort in Scripture points to the motive of compassion or identification with another and with the other's needs, which in turn leads to acts of mercy.

Help and comfort are descriptions of God's love. Another purpose of marriage, therefore, is to be an incarnation of God's unending, unmerited, unconditional, sacrificial, reconciling love. To be able to love in this manner is a consequence of one's spiritual life. It is because we have known and experienced God's love that we can love each other in this manner. Your life together is to be a testimony to the nature and character of God's love.

Children and Their Nurture
Christianity has from the beginning contended that both singleness and marriage are holy. Both states provide ways to serve God and reach the end of human life. By so doing the church established that getting married and having children were not a necessity or a "natural" event. The choice to get married and, if it is God's will, to have children had deep spiritual and moral significance.

I once wrote a book entitled *Will our Children Have Faith?*; a colleague later wrote an article "Will Our Faith Have Children?" There may be faithful, moral reasons not to have children, but we must be sure that they are not decisions made in despair about the future or for selfish reasons. Children are a sign that life, in spite of its hardship and tedium, is worthwhile. Children are a symbol of hope, hope in God about the future. And children represent our confidence that our faith has merit and can meet the needs of future generations.

Before the marriage celebration you will be required to sign the following declaration: "We, A.B. and C.D., desiring to receive the blessing of Holy Matrimony in the Church, do solemnly declare that we hold marriage to be a lifelong union of husband and wife as it is set forth in the Book of Common Prayer.

"We believe that the union of husband and wife, in heart, body and mind, is intended for their mutual joy; for the help and comfort to one another in prosperity and adversity; and, when it is God's will, for the procreation of children and their nurture in the knowledge and love of the Lord.

"And we do engage ourselves, so far as in us lies, to make our utmost effort to establish and to seek God's help thereto."

The Episcopal Church's understanding of the marriage covenant is founded upon an understanding of life in the reign of God and the fact that we live in between the times, between the already and not yet of God's reign. Therefore, while we need to strive, with God's help, to live lives that are based on life in God's reign, there may be circumstances that prevent us from doing so. For example, in the case of physical or mental abuse, to keep the marriage covenant would be destructive to a person's life, making divorce an option. When things are not going well, however, divorce should not be the first option we consider. In the Canons of the Episcopal Church on marriage we read, "When marital unity is imperiled by dissension, it shall be the duty of either or both parties, before contemplating legal action, to lay the matter before a Member of the Clergy; and it shall be the duty of such Member of the Clergy to labor that the parties may be reconciled." For, insofar as divorce is the breaking of a covenant promise, it is a sin. But like all sins, divorce is forgivable and God grants us another opportunity to demonstrate that with God's help we can maintain a covenant.

Marriage as a Sacrament

Another way to interpret the opening address on the meaning and purpose of marriage is to explain that from the church's point of view, marriage is a sacrament—that is, a sign through which the lives of a man and a woman united in Holy Matrimony testify to the presence of a gracious God who never gives up on us, who forgives us when we hurt our relationship, who seeks to give us what we need rather than what we deserve, and who accepts us as we are and desires the best for us.

Unlike the culture, the church teaches little about romantic love or love as an affection. It questions marriages founded primarily upon common interests, mutual advantage, contractual agreements, or sexual attraction. The church cares first about the character of the two persons who wish to receive the blessing of the church on their marriage, namely, whether or not they are capable of sustaining the kind of relationship upon which the keeping of promises is founded even if romantic love dries up and what originally attracted them to each other is no longer present.

At the celebration and blessing of a marriage, the church gathers for an amazing and awesome event: to witness two persons promise to love one another with a love measured by the kind of love God has for each of us, so that their life together might be a sacrament of God's grace, God's loving presence and action in human life and history.

"Dwell in my love," says Jesus, and then, "Love one another as I have loved you" (John 15:9). These words originally addressed to the disciples of Jesus are also addressed to those who seek God's blessing on their marriage: "Love one another as I have loved you, but first dwell in my love." This necessity explains why the church recommends that we celebrate the Eucharist at a wedding. We celebrate the Eucharist so as to make us aware of God's love, a love that is essential to the keeping of the marriage promise to love as God loves.

At the celebration and blessing of a marriage the church charges those participating in the sacrament with the awesome responsibility of being a sacrament of God's love, reminding us that the resource for the keeping of this promise is to be found in the church and its sacraments.

Holy Scripture and Marriage

The church has recommended particular lessons from Holy Scripture to be read and commented upon at the celebration and blessing of a marriage. These passages also provide a foundation for comprehending the church's understanding of marriage. What follows are those lessons and a brief commentary.

The Old Testament
Genesis 1:26–28

Then God said, "Let us make humankind in our image, according to our likeness; and let them have dominion over the fish of the sea, and over the birds of the air, and over the cattle, and over all the wild animals of the earth, and over every creeping thing that creeps upon the earth." So God created humankind in his image, in the image of God he created them; male and female he created them. God blessed them, and God said to them, "Be fruitful and multiply, and fill the earth and subdue it; and have dominion over the fish of the sea and over the birds of the air and over every living thing that moves upon the earth."

In this first account of creation, God births an orderly world out of original chaos and assigns a prominent place to human beings, who are in the image and likeness of their creator. To be in the image of God is to have the capacity to live in a loving and faithful relationship with God. To be in the likeness of God is to have the ability to know and do God's will.

In this account God also differentiates humanity into male and female so that humans might reproduce their kind, nurture them as God's dependent children, and become God's stewards of the natural world.

We human beings, in our uniqueness, therefore, have been en-
trusted with the responsibility of living in a faithful relationship
with God, with our true self (the self that is in the image and likeness of God), with all people, and with the natural world.

Genesis 2:4–9,15–24

*These are the generations of the heavens and the earth when they
were created. In the day that the LORD God made the earth and the
heavens, when no plant of the field was yet in the earth and no herb of
the field had yet sprung up—for the LORD God had not caused it to
rain upon the earth, and there was no one to till the ground; but a
stream would rise from the earth, and water the whole face of the
ground—then the LORD God formed man from the dust of the ground,
and breathed into his nostrils the breath of life; and the man became a
living being. And the LORD God planted a garden in Eden, in the east;
and there he put the man whom he had formed. Out of the ground the
LORD God made to grow every tree that is pleasant to the sight and
good for food, the tree of life also in the midst of the garden, and the
tree of the knowledge of good and evil. The LORD God took the man
and put him in the garden of Eden to till it and keep it. And the LORD
God commanded the man, "You may freely eat of every tree of the
garden; but of the tree of the knowledge of good and evil you shall not
eat, for in the day that you eat of it you shall die." Then the LORD God
said, "It is not good that the man should be alone; I will make him a
helper as his partner." So out of the ground the LORD God formed
every animal of the field and every bird of the air, and brought them to
the man to see what he would call them; and whatever the man called
every living creature, that was its name. The man gave names to all
cattle, and to the birds of the air, and to every animal of the field; but
for the man there was not found a helper as his partner. So the LORD
God caused a deep sleep to fall upon the man, and he slept; then he
took one of his ribs and closed up its place with flesh. And the rib that
the LORD God had taken from the man he made into a woman and
brought her to the man. Then the man said, "This at last is bone of my
bones and flesh of my flesh; this one shall be called Woman, for out of
Man this one was taken." Therefore a man leaves his father and his
mother and clings to his wife, and they become one flesh.*

In this second account of creation, God's first act is the birthing of human beings. As such, we come from the ground but have God's life breathed into us; we thereby became human beings who must live in a dependent relationship with God. This implies that we are never to desire the knowledge that will result in our distrusting or excluding God, giving us the false impression that we are independent beings who can manage nature, history, our political and economic systems, or our own lives.

This lesson also establishes marriage as a new manifestation of the created order, namely, the reality of one flesh. The sexual relationship of a man and a woman within the context of marriage is an outward expression of an inward reality, their union in heart and mind. Sexual intercourse, while restricted to this monogamous relationship, does not create the intimacy of the relationship but is a consequence of this intimacy.

Tobit 8:5b–8
"Blessed are you, O God of our ancestors and blessed is your name in all generations forever. Let the heavens and the whole creation bless you forever. You made Adam, and for him you made his wife Eve as a helper and support. From the two of them the human race has sprung. You said, 'It is not good that the man should be alone; let us make a helper for him like himself.' I now am taking this kinswoman of mine, not because of lust, but with sincerity. Grant that she and I may find mercy and that we may grow old together."

Tobit is a delightful biblical story of an ancient Jewish family and the adventure of a dutiful son who goes on a journey, in the company of an angel, to find a bride and then returns with her to help heal and restore his family's life. Just prior to this passage, the angel Raphael has instructed Tobiah to call on Sarah, his bride, to join him in prayer. This passage contains their prayer. It begins with a blessing, the usual invocation found in all Jewish prayers, and continues as a prayer of thanksgiving for their love and marriage.

It is through their trust in God and their fidelity to one another that the power of God's love is revealed in their lives. The author of this Apocryphal story would have every engaged and married couple acknowledge the importance of prayer and the need to open themselves to God's loving presence and action in their relationship.

Song of Solomon 2:10–13, 8:6–7

My beloved speaks and says to me: "Arise, my love, my fair one, and come away; for now the winter is past, the rain is over and gone. The flowers appear on the earth; the time of singing has come, and the voice of the turtledove is heard in our land. The fig tree puts forth its figs, and the vines are in blossom; they give forth fragrance. Arise, my love, my fair one, and come away. . . . Set me as a seal upon your heart, as a seal upon your arm; for love is strong as death, passion fierce as the grave. Its flashes are flashes of fire, a raging flame. Many waters cannot quench love, neither can floods drown it. If offered for love all the wealth of one's house, it would be utterly scorned.

This book, known also as the Song of Songs in the Hebrew Bible, is filled with rapturous expressions of tender emotion and human sexual love. While both Jewish and Christian tradition have found another level of meaning in this book— the love between God and God's people—it is essentially a collection of wedding songs intended to be used in the marriage ceremony.

This passage begins as a delightful song about the reality and joy of romantic love and ends with an acknowledgment that only the power of true love, love as an act of the will, can sustain a marriage over time.

The Psalms
Psalm 67
May God be gracious to us and bless us and make his face to shine upon us, Selah that your way may be known upon earth, your saving power among all nations. Let the peoples praise you, O God; let all the peoples praise you. Let the nations be glad and sing for joy, for you judge the peoples with equity and guide the nations upon earth. Selah Let the peoples praise you, O God; let all the peoples praise you. The earth has yielded its increase; God, our God, has blessed us. May God continue to bless us; let all the ends of the earth revere him.

This psalm is a prayer acknowledging that our gladness and joy are a testimony to God's love and mercy; it therefore requests God's blessing.

Psalm 127
Unless the LORD builds the house, those who build it labor in vain. Unless the LORD guards the city, the guard keeps watch in vain. It is in vain that you rise up early and go late to rest, eating the bread of anxious toil; for he gives sleep to his beloved. Sons are indeed a heritage from the LORD, the fruit of the womb a reward. Like arrows in the hand of a warrior are the sons of one's youth. Happy is the man who has his quiver full of them. He shall not be put to shame when he speaks with his enemies in the gate.

This psalm is a reminder that it is God who establishes families and that children are not our possessions, but a gift from God for us to love and nurture.

Psalm 128
Happy is everyone who fears the LORD, who walks in his ways. You shall eat the fruit of the labor of your hands; you shall be happy, and it shall go well with you. Your wife will be like a fruitful vine within your house; your children will be like olive shoots around your table. Thus shall the man be blessed who fears the LORD. The LORD bless you from Zion. May you see the prosperity of Jerusalem all the days of your life. May you see your children's children. Peace be upon Israel!

This psalm is a statement of faith that the ever reliable and loving God will always bless those who show respect and reverence to God.

The New Testament
1 Corinthians 13:1–13

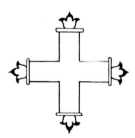

If I speak in the tongues of mortals and of angels, but do not have love, I am a noisy gong or a clanging cymbal. And if I have prophetic powers, and understand all mysteries and all knowledge, and if I have all faith, so as to remove mountains, but do not have love, I am nothing. If I give away all my possessions, and if I hand over my body so that I may boast, but do not have love, I gain nothing. Love is patient; love is kind; love is not envious or boastful or arrogant or rude. It does not insist on its own way; it is not irritable or resentful; it does not rejoice in wrongdoing, but rejoices in the truth. It bears all things, believes all things, hopes all things, endures all things. Love never ends. But as for prophecies, they will come to an end; as for tongues, they will cease; as for knowledge, it will come to an end. For we know only in part, and we prophesy only in part; but when the complete comes, the partial will come to an end. When I was a child, I spoke like a child, I thought like a child, I reasoned like a child; when I became an adult, I put an end to childish ways. For now we see in a mirror, dimly, but then we will see face to face. Now I know only in part; then I will know fully, even as I have been fully known. And now faith, hope, and love abide, these three; and the greatest of these is love.

In this letter to the community of faith in Corinth, St. Paul explains that the love of God has been poured into their hearts through the Holy Spirit. This love is a gift that makes possible their living a life of love, a love that is an act of the will rather than an emotion or conviction.

Paul describes the nature and character of this love in detail and then concludes that with the help of God they can will to love each other in this manner. It is this same love that is to characterize the married life. Indeed, if a marriage is to succeed, it will be because both husband and wife have loved each other in this manner.

Ephesians 5:1-2,21-33

Therefore be imitators of God, as beloved children, and live in love, as Christ loved us and gave himself up for us, a fragrant offering and sacrifice to God. Be subject to one another out of reverence for Christ. Wives, be subject to your husbands as you are to the Lord. For the husband is the head of the wife just as Christ is the head of the church, the body of which he is the Savior. Just as the church is subject to Christ, so also wives ought to be, in everything, to their husbands. Husbands, love your wives, just as Christ loved the church and gave himself up for her, in order to make her holy by cleansing her with the washing of water by the word, so as to present the church to himself in splendor, without a spot or wrinkle or anything of the kind--yes, so that she may be holy and without blemish. In the same way, husbands should love their wives as they do their own bodies. He who loves his wife loves himself. For no one ever hates his own body, but he nourishes and tenderly cares for it, just as Christ does for the church, because we are members of his body. "For this reason a man will leave his father and mother and be joined to his wife, and the two will become one flesh." This is a great mystery, and I am applying it to Christ and the church. Each of you, however, should love his wife as himself, and a wife should respect her husband.

This passage from a letter addressed to the church in Ephesus was likely written by an unknown author at a date later than those of Paul and then circulated to churches throughout the area. As such, it reflects views of the early church as it struggled to be accepted in a world that no longer was considered to be coming to an end. At this time it was believed that there was a hierarchy in the natural order and that marriage needed to reflect the pyramidal structure of society and the cultural values of the day.

While this passage can be interpreted in helpful ways, it has been misused through the years to suppress and oppress women and therefore may not be useful in our day. Seen in its best light, it speaks of a life of mutual respect and the duty to seek each other's good. As such, it implies that a husband and wife are to love themselves and each other equally, thereby forming a relationship like that of Christ and the church, namely, of mutual, self-giving love.

Ephesians 3:14–19
For this reason I bow my knees before the Father, from whom every family in heaven and on earth takes its name. I pray that, according to the riches of his glory, he may grant that you may be strengthened in your inner being with power through his Spirit, and that Christ may dwell in your hearts through faith, as you are being rooted and grounded in love. I pray that you may have the power to comprehend, with all the saints, what is the breadth and length and height and depth, and to know the love of Christ that surpasses knowledge, so that you may be filled with all the fullness of God.

In this passage addressed to the church in Ephesus the author shares a prayer he has offered up for them. In it he prays that they will be strengthened in their innermost selves with the power of the Holy Spirit and that Christ will dwell in their hearts. He then petitions that they, being rooted and grounded in God's love, might fully comprehend all the dimensions of true love and be empowered to share that love with each other. This represents a beautiful prayer to be offered for those who are about to enter the covenant of marriage.

Colossians 3:12–17
As God's chosen ones, holy and beloved, clothe yourselves with compassion, kindness, humility, meekness, and patience. Bear with one another and, if anyone has a complaint against another, forgive each other; just as the Lord has forgiven you, so you also must forgive. Above all, clothe yourselves with love, which binds everything together in perfect harmony. And let the peace of Christ rule in your hearts, to which indeed you were called in the one body. And be thankful. Let the word of Christ dwell in you richly; teach and admonish one another in all wisdom; and with gratitude in your hearts sing psalms, hymns, and spiritual songs to God. And whatever you do, in word or deed, do everything in the name of the Lord Jesus, giving thanks to God the Father through him.

In this passage we are reminded of our baptismal vows and covenant and the new way of life that has been made possible for us. Through this sacramental action we are made aware that our lives have been transformed by God's action in Christ and that we have been empowered to love as God loves. As God's chosen ones we have a responsibility to manifest this life of love so that others might know what is possible for them also.

In this case, it serves as a reminder to husbands and wives that they are called to have Christ-like characters and live virtuous lives. Marriage is a school for spiritual growth, and participating in the liturgical life of the church is the key to a life together that is faithful to the Gospel.

1 John 4:7–16

Beloved, let us love one another, because love is from God; everyone who loves is born of God and knows God. Whoever does not love does not know God, for God is love. God's love was revealed among us in this way: God sent his only Son into the world so that we might live through him. In this is love, not that we loved God but that he loved us and sent his Son to be the atoning sacrifice for our sins. Beloved, since God loved us so much, we also ought to love one another. No one has ever seen God; if we love one another, God lives in us, and his love is perfected in us. By this we know that we abide in him and he in us, because he has given us of his Spirit. And we have seen and do testify that the Father has sent his Son as the Savior of the world. God abides in those who confess that Jesus is the Son of God, and they abide in God. So we have known and believe the love that God has for us. God is love, and those who abide in love abide in God, and God abides in them.

In this passage John proclaims that God is love. He explains that what we say and how we live are inseparably linked. Our faith is revealed in our lives. Our spiritual and moral lives are one. How we live is a natural consequence of how we experience God. God's unconditional, unmerited, reconciling love is prior to our response in which we are to love in a similar manner.

As a consequence of our experience of God's love we learn how we are to love. God's love also both inspires and enables us to love accordingly. Because we know God's love, we can love our spouse even when he or she is so needy for love that reciprocating it is impossible.

The Gospel
Matthew 5:1–10
When Jesus saw the crowds, he went up the mountain; and after he sat down, his disciples came to him. Then he began to speak, and taught them, saying:
  "Blessed are the poor in spirit, for theirs is the kingdom of heaven.
  "Blessed are those who mourn, for they will be comforted.
  "Blessed are the meek, for they will inherit the earth.
  "Blessed are those who hunger and thirst for righteousness, for they
      will be filled.
  "Blessed are the merciful, for they will receive mercy.
  "Blessed are the pure in heart, for they will see God.
  "Blessed are the peacemakers, for they will be called children of God.
  "Blessed are those who are persecuted for righteousness' sake, for
      theirs is the kingdom of heaven.

In this passage Jesus describes the character traits of those who choose to follow in his way. We read this passage in a marriage ceremony to remind ourselves that one of the purposes of marriage is to help each other experience and practice these virtues.

The Christian way of life is one in which we are called to strive to live totally dependent upon God; we are to strive to be sensitive to the world's sin and sorry for our participation in it; we are to strive to never nurse anger; we are to strive to have as our life's goal to live in a right relationship with God; we are to strive to be caring, compassionate persons; we are to strive to live with motives that are as pure as our acts; we are to strive to be forgiving, reconciling people; and we are to strive to be willing to pay whatever the cost to do the will of God.

Matthew 5:13–16
"You are the salt of the earth; but if salt has lost its taste, how can its saltiness be restored? It is no longer good for anything, but is thrown out and trampled under foot. "You are the light of the world. A city built on a hill cannot be hid. No one after lighting a lamp puts it under the bushel basket, but on the lampstand, and it gives light to all in the house. In the same way, let your light shine before others, so that they may see your good works and give glory to your Father in heaven.

One purpose of marriage is to help each other grow in the Christian faith and life. Here Jesus speaks of two aspects of this life of faith, namely our resemblance to salt and light (Matthew 5:13-14). Salt is valued and symbolic of purity. To be an example of purity is to be free

from sin. Salt is a preserving, cleansing, healing substance, and so is the Christian to have a cleansing, antiseptic influence on life. Just as salt lends flavor to things, so the Christian is to bring joy to others.

And just as Jesus was light to the world, so are we to be light. Light helps us to see, and as light we are to make visible God's presence and action in human life and history. Light can be used as a guide, and we are to give witness to others and aid them as they follow in the way of Jesus. Light helps us to see, and we are to help others perceive what is good and provide a warning of that which is not.

Furthermore, we are to do all this without drawing attention to ourselves. Rather, we are to make sure that others know that this life can be lived only through the grace of God.

Matthew 7:21, 24–29

"Not everyone who says to me, 'Lord, Lord,' will enter the kingdom of heaven, but only the one who does the will of my Father in heaven. "Everyone then who hears these words of mine and acts on them will be like a wise man who built his house on rock. The rain fell, the floods came, and the winds blew and beat on that house, but it did not fall, because it had been founded on rock. And everyone who hears these words of mine and does not act on them will be like a foolish man who built his house on sand. The rain fell, and the floods came, and the winds blew and beat against that house, and it fell--and great was its fall!" Now when Jesus had finished saying these things, the crowds were astounded at his teaching, for he taught them as one having authority, and not as their scribes.

Jesus reminds us that as husband and wife we are metaphorically to build our home on a solid spiritual and moral foundation. To do this we need to take time to be quiet and listen for God's word to us. We need to meditate on Scripture. And we need prayerfully to discern the will of God.

But just as all insights have implications, we need not only to know how to discern the will of God, but to *do* the will of God.

In your married life, therefore, you are to help each other strive to know and do the will of God.

Mark 10:6–9,13–16

But from the beginning of creation, 'God made them male and female.' 'For this reason a man shall leave his father and mother and be joined to his wife, and the two shall become one flesh.' So they are no longer two, but one flesh. Therefore what God has joined together, let no one separate." People were bringing little children to him in order that he might touch them; and the disciples spoke sternly to them. But when Jesus saw this, he was indignant and said to them, "Let the little children come to me; do not stop them; for it is to such as these that the kingdom of God belongs. Truly I tell you, whoever does not receive the kingdom of God as a little child will never enter it." And he took them up in his arms, laid his hands on them, and blessed them.

Here Jesus unites two teachings. The first is that as followers of Jesus, you are called to a life of fidelity, of faithfulness to each other for a lifetime.

The second is a reminder that this fidelity is possible only if you both live with a childlike trust and dependence on God, for while with God all things are possible without God's help we can do nothing.

John 15:9–12

As the Father has loved me, so I have loved you; abide in my love. If you keep my commandments, you will abide in my love, just as I have kept my Father's commandments and abide in his love. I have said these things to you so that my joy may be in you, and that your joy may be complete. "This is my commandment, that you love one another as I have loved you."

Here Jesus reminds us that in the marriage relationship we are to love one another with a love measured by the love God has for us, a love that is possible only if both husband and wife dwell in God's love.

To experience this love you will need to develop a spiritual discipline that includes personal prayer and corporate worship. It is especially important to participate regularly in the Eucharist and the sacraments of reconciliation and healing.

Marriage is About Love and The Promise To Love

Two persons become married when each pledges himself or herself to the other, consenting to a particular relationship with this person alone and thereby reserving for each other those acts that engender, nourish, and establish a unique unity of "two that are one." It is not that you cease to be two unique, distinctive selves but that a new dimension of human life is established, namely a mysterious intimacy of souls (composed of a body, mind, and spirit).

This unique relationship combines three expressions of love: erotic love, friendship love, and charity love.

Erotic love is passionate sexual love. It is different from lust in that lust turns a subject into an object for our manipulation. Pornography is one manifestation of lust, and so is adultery. Erotic love, which is manifested in coitus, a unity of body, can only be with one person striving for fusion with the other through physical expression. Healthy erotic love never precedes friendship love; it follows it.

Friendship love is reciprocal affection and intimacy of mind and spirit. It is founded on common values, interests, needs, experiences, hopes and dreams, and mutual benefit. While we can be friendly with many people, we can be friends with very few. Friendship love takes time and commitment. It is my experience that a married person cannot have a friendship with a person of the opposite sex. Your mate must be your only real friend. To have another will take time away from this primary friendship. Further, the intimacy that results from such a friendship tempts us to express it physically, an act that would break the marriage covenant. You can have, however, a friendship with someone of your own sex, but the number of such friendships and the time required of these friendships must not get in the way of your primary friendship; rather, such relationships and the time they require should enhance and enliven one's friendship with one's spouse.

Charity love is not an affection; it is an act of the will. It is unconditional, unmerited, unending action of love that seeks the other's good. Charity love does not require us to give up loving ourselves. We are to love ourselves and all others equally. However, we are to give up selfish love, love which only cares about our own needs, our own good. Charity love is to consider the needs and good of one's spouse as equal to and as important as one's own. It means to will such love for our spouse whether or not at any one moment they will it for us. It is charity love that we promise each other in the marriage rite. It is a love made possible by our love relationship with God.

Romance, as I understand it, combines all these expressions of love; it can last a lifetime and indeed grow in depth. But romantic love is something else. It is natural but it does not last or grow. Nor will it sustain or strengthen a marriage. Romantic love is not a sufficient justification for marriage. We can all fall in love, that is, experience romantic love, with many people, but only a very few of those we can fall in romantic love with will we ever be able to live with for a lifetime.

Romance can and should continue through a lifetime. But romantic love is not real love and cannot be sustained. It is a psychological, affective attachment that draws us to another. We need to look below the surface of romantic love and name what really attracts us to another person. We must not enter marriage with blinders on. Opposites attract but later repel. To seek completeness in your own life by finding someone who has qualities in which you are deficient will become a problem in the relationship later when one or both parties grow and develop in that area and therefore no longer need the other for wholeness. This can be a bigger problem when people marry young, that is, before they have matured and know who they are and what kind of persons they can, need, and desire to live with till death.

Romantic love also assumes that the one you love can change, will change, or that you can change him or her. That assumption is wrong, and so is the assumption that the one you romantically love cannot change, will not change, or that you can stop him or her from changing. We always marry three persons: the person we think we've married (always partially a delusion), the person we really have married, and the person our spouse will become.

Building A
Happy, Healthy Marriage

Marriage relationships have changed a great deal over the years. There was a time when marriages were arranged and love as an affection was not considered important. Most everyone married at a young age, had a large family, and lived in the same home or town as one's grandparents and parents, brothers and sisters, aunts and uncles, single and married. These relationships were essential to survival, security, and identity. Clear roles were established for men and women as well as each generation. Adultery may have been common, but divorces were both socially condemned and legally difficult to acquire. In those days marriages as contracts might not be happy, but they were not in danger of being dissolved.

Today people choose whom they will marry, and love as an affection plays a significant role. People tend to get married later and have smaller families. The nuclear family is dominant and the generations both mobile and geographically separated. No longer are there clear and established roles for men and women, and marriage is no longer important to survival, security, or identity. Now marriages focus on the quality of the relationship. Divorce in such a society typically is more acceptable and easier to acquire.

Nevertheless, lifelong, fulfilling, life-giving marriages are as possible as ever. To experience a healthy marriage you need to begin by thinking carefully about the meaning and purpose of marriage and your readiness to make the promises required of marriage.

You also will need to be committed to working intentionally together on your relationship for a lifetime, for there is nothing natural about being and remaining married. Further, you will need the support of others and, on occasion, professional help. Experiencing difficulties and problems in a marriage is normal and natural. Many cannot be resolved without the help of a clergyperson or marriage counselor. It is important to get assistance early, before the relationship is too broken to be repaired. All couples should consider going annually for a "check-up."

We have learned that successful marriages are composed of the following traits:
1. Good communications.
2. Affirmation and support for each other's growth.
3. Shared responsibilities.
4. Mutuality of decision making.
5. Established trust through telling the truth and keeping your word.
6. Enjoyment of each other and a preference to do things together.
7. Concern for others and participation together in community service.
8. Shared common values and a vision for your life together.
9. A common faith and shared life in a community of faith.
10. A shared spiritual life.

Interestingly, it is this shared spiritual life that is the foundation and key to a happy, healthy marriage. Therefore, if you have a shared spiritual life, you can live through difficult days and your marriage survive rough times. If you do not, there is not much to keep the marriage together or sustain it during these times.

The Spiritual Life

The spiritual life is ordinary, everyday life lived in an ever deepening and loving relationship with God. And it is this spiritual life that shapes and informs our moral life, that is, ordinary everyday life lived in an ever deepening and loving relationship to our true self (the self that is in the image and likeness of God), to all people, and to the natural world. It is the moral life that is the test of the spiritual life. If our relationship to self, neighbor, and nature is to be healthy, then our relationship to God must be healthy. If you experience difficulty in your marriage relationship, there is always a spiritual component that needs to be addressed along with the relationship itself. For example, we all need to be loved and to experience love if we are to love another. But there are times when we are needy for love but so drained that we have no love to return. Since we cannot give what we have not received, we need to turn to God and open ourselves to God's love so that we can love without needing to have it returned immediately.

The spiritual life has a great deal to do with our images of God. It is easy to forget that our images of God influence our behavior. There is always a direct relationship between our faith (our perceptions of God) and our lives. If we image a God of judgment and retribution, we will more than likely believe and behave in terms of being critical of others and wanting to make sure that people get what they deserve. If we image a God of love and reconciliation, we will more than likely believe and behave in terms of trying to understand others and making sure that people get what they need. Unless a couple shares common images of God, the marriage will be threatened.

One of the most important decisions you will make is the choice of a congregation with which to belong and worship. You need to discuss how you plan to participate in that congregation's life and the amount of money and time you will pledge to support its ministry. These conversations need to take place before your marriage.

It is important that you agree on such matters or they will become divisive later on. It is a cliché to say that the couple that prays together stays together, but it most often is true. Sharing life together in a congregation will not guarantee a happy and fulfilling marriage, but it surely will provide a foundation for one.

Prayer is best understood as anything you do that aids your relationship with God. Prayer can be a societal action such as being with and serving the poor, the homeless, the sick, and the needy. Prayer can be contemplative action, such as repeating a centering prayer, "Gentle, loving God, the mother of my soul, hold me as your own," over and over again with your breathing. Prayer can be the formal repeating of a daily office. Prayer can be composed of spontaneous words addressed to God: "God, I love you because . . ."; "God, I thank you for . . ."; "God I am sorry that . . ."; "God I desire for . . .," etc. Prayer can be meditation on Scripture. Prayer can be two minutes of silence every hour to be conscious of God's presence in your life. What is important is that together you establish a personal and corporate spiritual discipline for your lives. That is, establish a time, a place, and a means for working on your relationship with God.

The Book of Common Prayer can help you. Beginning on page 136, there are daily devotions for morning, noon, the early evening, and the close of the day. There is Daily Morning Prayer beginning on page 75; an Order of Service for Noonday beginning on page 103; Daily Evening Prayer beginning on page 115; and an Order for Compline, to be used before going to sleep, beginning on page 127. Ask your priest to help you to use these beautiful liturgies.

There is also an Order of Worship for the Evening beginning on page 108, which provides an outline for prayer before an evening meal. It could be used every evening, on Friday, Saturday, and/or Sunday evening as fits your married life. Used as part of saying grace and asking God's blessing on your food and life could be a wonderful way to begin developing a spiritual discipline.

One other important resource is the *Contemporary Office Book*, published by the Church Hymnal Corporation. Not only does it contain all the offices mentioned, it contains the assigned reading from Scripture for every day in the year. If you read these each day you will travel through the whole of Scripture every two years. Just prayerfully reading even one of the lessons each day will provide you with a foundation for a spiritual life.

If you wish, you might add another dimension to reading Scripture by participating in the following steps: Read the lesson slowly; enter into a word, a phrase, the story, or a character so that you might experience God's word; with God reflect on your experience so as to discover insights and their implications for your life; acknowledge the grace you need if you are to live out this implication; and open yourself so that God might give you that grace as his gift to you.

And last, every couple needs a Sabbath, but we must be careful not to confuse a day off from Sabbath. We all need a day off from work to do all those personal and family chores that cannot get done at other times, such as cleaning the yard, going to the store, catching up on work, or balancing the checkbook. Nevertheless, our spiritual life requires a day of Sabbath, a day to renew and refresh our love with God and each other. Every couple needs to declare that the world and its pressures must give way to the two of you and your marriage. Sabbath is a time for intimacy and romantic, unhurried sex; a time for rest and refreshment (dining rather than eating); a time for being together in playful ways (being rather than doing); and a time for God and prayer. A happy, healthy marriage has a Sabbath time each week.

Marriage as a School for the Spiritual Life

Marriage is a people-growing process. Just when two people begin to be independent of home and family and discover their own interests and needs, they surrender their independence and enter an interdependent (adult-to-adult) relationship. It is difficult to live in this sort of relationship, and so each week we need to take the time to digress into a extradependent (child-to-parent) relationship with God, who transforms us through nurture and nourishment, to return and live in a healthy, faithful relationship of intradependence as a married couple. Indeed, it can be the difficulties of living faithfully together as maturing persons in community that aid us to grow in our spiritual life.

To prepare yourself for a healthy married relationship it is important that during the engagement period you both spend a significant amount of nonromantic time together, spend time apart, spend time with each other's family and discuss your religious, political, economic, and social values. Do not forget that your future mate was influenced (negatively and/or positively) by his or her family and will continue to be. Remember that you will need to interact and relate to your mate's family throughout your married life. It is in more than one sense that you marry into another family.

Some questions to discuss might be the following: What are you looking for and hoping for in your marriage? About what are you most anxious? What do you like most about the person you are marrying? What do you not like as well? What do you like most and least in the family of the person you intend to marry? What have you come to appreciate more in the person you intend to marry as time has gone by? What do you like most about your-self? What do you not like as well? How have you changed in the last few years? What would you like to change in yourself and what help do you need? How are the two of you most different? How are you most alike? What are promises you have made in the past and broken? How did you deal with these broken prom-ises? Complete the following sentences: I believe I will be acting as a good husband/wife when . . . I believe you will be acting as a good husband/wife when . . . .

Marriage is a journey over time. It moves from a personal rela-tionship, to the birth and rearing of children, to a career or careers, to the empty nest, to retirement or second career

and to the death of one of you. At each of these transitions, as well as events such as an accident or sickness, and as a consequence of your each maturing, growing, and changing your needs, your marriage covenant needs to be reconstituted. There is in the Episcopal Church's *Book of Occasional Services* a beautiful liturgy for the reaffirmation of the marriage covenant. If the sacrament of mar-riage, like baptism, is something you live into, you need continually to work together in main-taining your marriage.

Baptism initiates us into the reign of God, and marriage for the baptized is a way of life that anticipates the coming of God's reign in its fullness. Jesus chose a wedding as the first signifi-cant event in his public life. At this event Jesus turned water into wine to signify that he came to make all things new, including marriage, to which he gave new meaning and purpose.

Marriage is for the sake of Christ, his Church, and the world. Marriage becomes idolatry when it is seen as an end in itself rather than a means. Family life is to be understood as a sign and witness to God's reign. When we observe how married people treat each other and behave in society, we should observe what life in God's reign looks like.

The married life is also a way into the reign of God. As such, it is an eschatological process, that is, a mere stepping stone on its way to a future goal. Insofar as this is true, marriage is experienced as incomplete and unfulfilled. It is marked by fidelity and a continuous striving, with God's help, to realize its potential. Marriage is a pilgrimage directed by God toward its final goal. It is a pilgrimage composed of many small deaths and resurrections, (the death of love of self alone, and the birth of love of self and another equally), of suffering and happiness (the experience of being estranged and reconciled).

As with all journeys, there can be roadblocks. There is a natural urge to complete oneself in another, which is why opposites attract. When this occurs, we call the experience love. But it is a love that may appear to be a losing of oneself in another and is thus self-serving. It is an experience of love that cannot continue over time, indeed must change if one is to mature and find wholeness and health in oneself rather than in another. Mature love is equally concerned with the growth and fulfillment of the other as oneself and is more concerned with the relationship than with one's own needs.

Another roadblock to a fulfilling marriage is seeing marriage as a means to escape a situation we do not like, such as an unhappy home, or to acquire a situation we do like, such as someone to take care of us. You need to make sure that your relationship with the one you intend to marry is more important to you than any problem the relationship might solve.

A Walk Through the Marriage Rite

Secure a copy of the 1979 *Book of Common Prayer* and turn to page 422. Read the rubrics concerning the service. Then, after reading the words in the liturgy, read the commentary that follows.

(Note also on page 433 a rite for the Blessing of a Civil Marriage, and on page 435 an Order for Marriage, which makes possible the creation of your own liturgy. However, notice that you may not write your own vows if you desire the church's blessing. On page 437 there are some additional directions on marriage.)

Please remember that there are local customs and preferences of your priest that need to be honored. Therefore, what follows are only suggestions and possibilities to be considered if approved. Remember, all music must be approved by the organist and priest. There is some music that while appropriate at the wedding reception is not appropriate in the marriage liturgy.

The Entrance
While in most weddings an organ voluntary is played during the procession of the wedding party, an alternative of instrumental music, a hymn, psalm, or sung anthem is possible.

Typically, the priest, the groom, and the best man come in from the side, the families of the bride and groom having been seated earlier. Then the ushers two by two come down the aisle, followed by the bridesmaids one by one, the maid of honor, and finally the bride and her father or father's representative. But there are possibilities such as a crucifer and candles followed by the priest, the best man and groom, and then as before. It is also appropriate for the families to be part of the procession, with the mother and father walking in with both the bride and the groom.

Unlike in the past, when a bride, like property, was given away by her fathers, who stood behind her until that was done, now the father typically delivers his daughter to the groom and goes to his pew.

THE BETROTHAL

The Exhortation
While it is tradition to stand for this part of the liturgy, it is also appropriate for those gathered, except the bridal party, to sit so they can see and therefore more fully participate.

The priest now establishes what we are about to do, namely witness and bless a marriage, that is, a covenant relationship of willed love, a relationship that has its foundation in Holy Scripture.

He continues by explaining the purpose of this relationship, namely, for the couple to support and encourage each other in their spiritual life, to be a symbol of how God loves all people, and to be open to bearing or adopting and nurturing children in that love.

The Charge
This first segment of the liturgy is composed of elements found in early betrothals. Notice that the responses, "I will," are in the future tense.

As an historic act both the couple and those gathered are asked a legal-moral question concerning whether anyone has reason to believe that this couple should not be married.

The Declaration of Consent

Then, beginning with the woman, both of you are asked if you understand and accept the life-long relationship to which you intend to commit yourselves. Within this declaration is one of the most significant changes from earlier liturgies. No longer does the bride promise to obey and serve her husband. Rather, the principles of equality and mutuality are established.

The question "Will you have" is not a question of ownership or possession but rather a question about being one in body, mind, and spirit through a unique covenantal relationship based on love as an act of the will that seeks the other's good, that encourages and supports and cares for the other's needs, and that will hold each other in esteem under all circumstances, for a lifetime.

The Pledge and Support

Importantly, the family, friends, and community that have gathered to witness this holy event are asked for their promise of support. There is nothing natural or easy about keeping the marriage covenant. We need all the help we can get. When choosing a bridesmaid and best man, as well as others in the wedding party, it is important to consider who will be able to provide the best support and help to you maintain a healthy, faithful marriage.

The Presentation

In place of the bride's being given away, it is now the custom for the priest to ask, "Who presents this woman and this man to be married to each other?" and for all the members of both families to reply, "I do." There are other options that are less equalitarian, but it is an important issue for which you need to make a decision.

A hymn and anthem may be placed here, especially if there was no processional hymn.

THE MINISTRY OF THE WORD

The ministry of the word is introduced by a collect that asks God's grace, God's loving presence and action in your lives, a grace that alone will make it possible for you to keep your promises and vows.

It is now appropriate to have an Old Testament lesson, a Psalm, a New Testament lesson, a hymn, and then a Gospel lesson followed by a homily. The Old Testament lesson and New Testament lesson may be read by a member of the family or wedding party. Other readings may be added, with the permission of the priest. If the Eucharist is to follow, the Gospel is to be read by a priest or deacon. During this part of the liturgy the wedding party and congregation are to be seated.

THE MARRIAGE

The priest, the bride and groom, and the maid of honor and best man now proceed to the altar for the next part of the liturgy.

The groom faces the bride and takes her right hand. Either reciting from memory or aided by the priest, the groom enters into the marriage covenant and makes his solemn promise to keep that covenant forever. The couple drops hands, and the bride, taking the groom's right hand, promises the same.

These solemn vows begin with the words "In the name of God," thereby acknowledging God as the third party in the marriage and inviting God to provide all that is necessary so that the marriage might flourish and its purposes be fulfilled.

The Blessing of the Rings
The priest now asks God to bless the rings as a symbol of the
covenant promises that have been made, and then each of you,
beginning with the groom, places a ring on the other's finger as a
symbolic action of your entering into the holy relationship.

The Marriage Declaration
Wrapping his stole around your joined hands as a symbol of God's
"tying of the knot," the priest pronounces that you are now husband and wife and announces that as a consequence of what you
and God have done together, no one should, or should you permit
anyone doing anything that might in any way hurt or damage your
relationship.

The Prayers
The congregation now stands and a friend or member of the family
may lead the prayers, beginning with the Lord's Prayer, a prayer that
establishes a way of life for all people but, especially in this case, a
way of life that your marriage is intended to enhance and enliven.

Through the congregation's petitions God is asked to look with
favor upon your marriage; grant you all that is necessary for sup-
porting each other in your moral and spiritual lives; make it
possible that your wills and God's will, will be so joined that you
might grow in love; and to give you the grace to ask for and offer
forgiveness when you do anything to hurt your relationship. God
is also asked that your lives might reveal to the world the way God
loves; that you might receive the blessing of children; and that you
might give yourselves to loving others, especially those in need.
The prayers close with a petition for all those who are present and
married that their marriages might be enhanced and enlivened.

The Blessing of the Marriage
The couple now kneels and the priest pronounces God's blessing
on their marriage.

The Peace
The couple stands and the priest offers the kiss of peace, symbolic of reconciliation and unity, to the bride and groom; they then offer it to each other and to the maid of honor and best man. Then the couple proceeds to offer the kiss of peace to their families. The congregation joins in this act of reconciling love.

THE HOLY COMMUNION

The marriage liturgy anticipates that communion will follow to remind everyone that it is through your regular participation in this sacramental act that you will be granted the grace of an awareness of God's love, a grace necessary to sustain you in your marriage covenant of love. It is important for the priest to welcome all baptized persons to participate in this sacrament and to explain how we Episcopalians commune.

If the majority of those present will not be Christians, the bridal party might choose to have communion at the rehearsal, but it is never appropriate for the couple to have a private communion at the marriage ceremony. If there is no communion, the wedding party leaves the church with a hymn, anthem, or piece of instrumental music.

If communion is to follow, a hymn, anthem, or other piece of instrumental music is appropriate here, and it is customary for the bride and groom to go and take to the altar the bread and wine as their offering.

The Final Prayer and Exit
Following communion, there is a final prayer of thanksgiving for God's participation and action in this marriage. And then with a hymn, anthem, or other piece of instrumental music, the wedding party leaves, followed by the family and congregation.

Last Thoughts

There it is—my understanding of the Episcopal Church's meaning and purpose of marriage. I hope that you have found it informative and instrumental in stimulating a discussion between the two of you. You are about to make a tremendous change in your lives, and this change should not be entered into without serious reflection on the meaning and purpose of marriage and a commitment to living into its intentions. So be it, and Godspeed.